Famous Bible Passages

THE SECRET OF HAPPINESS

Matthew 5

A LION BOOK
Tring · Belleville · Sydney

Blessed are the poor in spirit,
for theirs is the kingdom of heaven.
Blessed are those who mourn,
for they will be comforted.
Blessed are the meek,
for they will inherit the earth.
Blessed are those who hunger and thirst
for righteousness, for they will be filled.
Blessed are the merciful,
for they will be shown mercy.
Blessed are the pure in heart,
for they will see God.
Blessed are the peacemakers,
for they will be called sons of God.
Blessed are those who are persecuted because of
righteousness, for theirs is the kingdom of heaven.
Blessed are you when people insult you, persecute
you and falsely say all kinds of evil against you
because of me.
Rejoice and be glad, because great is your reward
in heaven, for in the same way they persecuted
the prophets who were before you.

Matthew 5:3–12

*B*lessed are the poor in spirit

Jesus is the only one who could say 'blessed' with complete authority, for he is the Blessed One come from the world above to confer blessedness upon mankind. And his words were supported by deeds mightier than any performed on this earth by any other man.
A. W. Tozer

Humility is the very first letter in the alphabet of Christianity. We must begin low if we would build high.
J. C. Ryle

Jesus' blessings are for the poor, both in spirit and in substance. They know their need of God.
Jim Wallis

The man who is poor in spirit is the man who has realized that things mean nothing, and that God means everything.
William Barclay

God looks for spiritual riches. He wants us to let go of our worldly wealth, and invest our lives with him in heaven.
Andrew Knowles

God wants you to know him: wants to give you himself. . . If you really get into any kind of touch with him you will, in fact, be humble.
C. S. Lewis

A man begins to live before God only as he dies to his own nature.
Thomas Aquinas

*F*or theirs is the kingdom of heaven

Let us come to thy kingdom, where we will see thee face to face, and have perfect love, blessed company, and everlasting joy.

Francis of Assisi

The 'kingdom of heaven' is the rule of God through Christ. It is present wherever wills bow to him; it is future in complete realization in the heaven, from which it comes, and to which, like its King, it belongs, even while on earth.

Alexander MacLaren

This is what the high and lofty One says—
he who lives for ever, whose name is holy:
'I live in a high and holy place,
but also with him who is contrite and lowly in spirit,
to revive the spirit of the lowly
and to revive the heart of the contrite.'

Isaiah 57:15

He who became poor for us reigns over all creation. Therefore, if you become poor because he became poor, you will also reign because he is reigning.

Gregory of Nyssa

Having nothing, and yet possessing everything.

2 Corinthians 6:10

*B*lessed are those who mourn

The good man can find plenty to cause him sorrow and tears. He has only to consider himself or think of his neighbour, to realize that no one lives on this earth without distress; and the more closely he looks at himself, the more his grief increases. Our sins and failings give us good cause for sorrow and inner compunction.

Thomas à Kempis

A man who truly faces himself, and examines himself and his life, is a man who must of necessity mourn for his sins also, for the things he does.

Martyn Lloyd-Jones

By 'mourning' Jesus means doing without what the world calls peace and prosperity: he means refusing to be in tune with the world or to accommodate oneself to its standards. Such men mourn for the world, for its guilt, its fate, and its fortune. . . The world dreams of progress, of power and of the future but the disciples meditate on the end, the last judgement, and the coming of the kingdom.

Dietrich Bonhoeffer

*F*or they will be comforted

We can only know God well when we know our own sin.

Blaise Pascal

Godly sorrow brings repentance that leads to salvation and leaves no regret, but worldly sorrow brings death.

2 Corinthians 7:10

If we truly mourn, we shall rejoice, we shall be made happy, we shall be comforted. For it is when a man sees himself in this unutterable hopelessness that the Holy Spirit reveals unto him the Lord Jesus Christ as his perfect satisfaction.

Martyn Lloyd-Jones

Though it were enough for such mourners to receive pardon, yet he rests not his mercy only there, but makes them partakers of many comforts both here and hereafter. God's mercies are always greater than our troubles.

John Chrysostom

Those who mourn now are blessed, because they shall be comforted in the world without end.

Gregory of Nyssa

I saw a new heaven and a new earth; for the first heaven and the first earth had passed away, and the sea was no more. . . And I heard a loud voice from the throne saying, 'Behold, the dwelling of God is with men. He will dwell with them, and they shall be his people, and God himself will be with them; he will wipe away every tear from their eyes, and death shall be no more, neither shall there be mourning nor crying nor pain any more, for the former things have passed away.'

Revelation 21:1,3–4

*B*lessed are the meek

Have this mind among yourselves, which is yours in Christ Jesus, who, though he was in the form of God, did not count equality with God a thing to be grasped, but emptied himself, taking the form of a servant, being born in the likeness of men.

Philippians 2:5–7

The meek are those who yield before outbursts of wickedness and do not resist evil, but overcome evil with good.

Augustine

If a humble man is humiliated his peace is not disturbed, because he does not live by the world – his life depends on God.

Thomas à Kempis

The meek man . . . rests perfectly content to allow God to place his own values. He will be patient to wait for the day when everything will get its own price tag and real worth will come into its own. Then the righteous shall shine forth in the Kingdom of their Father. He is willing to wait for that day.

A. W. Tozer

*F*or they will inherit the earth

Those who now possess the earth by violence and injustice shall lose it, and those who here have utterly renounced it, who were meek to the point of the cross, shall rule the new earth . . . When the kingdom of heaven descends, the face of the earth will be renewed, and it will belong to the flock of Jesus.

Dietrich Bonhoeffer

The upright will inhabit the land,
and men of integrity will remain in it;
but the wicked will be cut off from the land,
and the treacherous will be rooted out of it.

Proverbs 2:21–22

The meek . . . although they may be deprived and disenfranchised by men, yet because they know what it is to live and reign with Christ, can enjoy and even 'possess' the earth which belongs to Christ. Then on the day of 'the regeneration' there will be 'new heavens and a new earth' for them to inherit.

John Stott

All things are yours, whether . . . the world or life or death or the present or the future, all are yours; and you are Christ's; and Christ is God's.

1 Corinthians 3:21–23

*B*lessed are those who hunger and thirst for righteousness

Righteousness . . . is the image of God, the mind which was in Christ Jesus.

John Wesley

People who enjoy the present things do not look for better ones. But if a man does not seek, he will not find what comes only to those who seek.

Gregory of Nyssa

It is better to be conscious of want than to be content.

Alexander MacLaren

The love of God is the love of goodness . . . To love God is to love what God is.

F. W. Robertson

Those who follow Jesus . . . are longing for the forgiveness of all sin, for complete renewal, for the renewal too of the earth and the full establishment of God's law.

Dietrich Bonhoeffer

We must become holy, not because we want to feel holy, but because Christ must be able to live his life fully in us.

Mother Teresa

---

*F*or they will be filled

He who pursues righteousness and kindness will find life and honour.
Proverbs 21:21

Ask, and it will be given you; seek, and you will find; knock, and it will be opened to you. For every one who asks receives, and he who seeks finds, and to him who knocks it will be opened.
Matthew 7:7–8

Jesus said to them, 'I am the bread of life; he who comes to me shall not hunger, and he who believes in me shall never thirst.'
John 6:35

O taste and see that the Lord is good!
Psalm 34:8

Almighty Master, you have created everything for the sake of your name, and have given men food and drink to enjoy that they may thank you. But to us you have given spiritual food and drink and eternal life through Jesus, your child.
The Didache

*B*lessed are the merciful

Mercy is a voluntary sorrow that joins itself to the sufferings of others.
Gregory of Nyssa

God cannot share his happiness with us if we are not willing to share his tastes, his character, his love, and his forgiveness.
Louis Evely

Mercy imitates God and disappoints Satan.
John Chrysostom

As God's chosen people, holy and dearly loved, clothe yourselves with compassion, kindness, humility, gentleness and patience. Bear with each other and forgive whatever grievances you may have against one another. Forgive as the Lord forgave you.
Colossians 3:12–13

God indeed is no respecter of persons, for he knows all things; and we ought to show mercy to all men.
Ambrose

*F*or they will be shown mercy

Who is a God like you,
who pardons sin and forgives the transgression
of the remnant of his inheritance?
You do not stay angry for ever
but delight to show mercy.

Micah 7:18

When the Son of Man comes in his glory, and all the angels with
him, he will sit on his throne in heavenly glory. All the nations will
be gathered before him, and he will separate the people one from
another as a shepherd separates the sheep from the goats . . . Then
the King will say to those on his right, 'Come, you are blessed by my
Father; take your inheritance, the kingdom prepared for you since
the creation of the world . . . I tell you the truth, whatever you did
for one of the least of these brothers of mine, you did for me.'

Matthew 25:31–32, 34, 40

What we are to others, God will be to us.

Charles Haddon Spurgeon

Blessed are the pure in heart

They are clean of heart who despise earthly things and always seek those of heaven, and who never cease to adore and contemplate the Lord God Living and True, with a pure heart and mind.

Francis of Assisi

We cannot see through a dirty windowpane; and we cannot see God through a heart sullied by selfish preoccupations and cares.

Louis Evely

The heart must be empty of all else, for God wishes to be its only possessor, and since he cannot be its only possessor without emptying it of all that is not himself, so too he cannot act therein or do his will.

Brother Lawrence

Purity . . . is accompanied with a great deal of pleasure. Whatsoever defiles the soul disturbs it too.

Henry Scougal

He that has a pure heart will never cease to pray; and he who will be constant in prayer shall know what it is to have a pure heart.

La Combe

---

*F*or they will see God

As we begin to focus upon God the things of the spirit will take shape before our inner eyes. . . . A new God-consciousness will seize upon us and we shall begin to taste and hear and inwardly feel the God who is our life and our all.

A. W. Tozer

Godliness is of value in every way, as it holds promise for the present life and also for the life to come.

1 Timothy 4:8

Only the pure in heart will see God, see him now with the eye of faith and see his glory in the hereafter, for only the utterly sincere can bear the dazzling vision in whose light the darkness of deceit must vanish and by whose fire all shams are burned up.

John Stott

Who shall ascend the hill of the Lord?
And who shall stand in his holy place?
He who has clean hands and a pure heart,
who does not lift up his soul to what is false,
and does not swear deceitfully.
He will receive blessing from the Lord,
and vindication from the God of his salvation.

Psalm 24:3–5

Only they will see God, who in this life have looked solely upon Jesus Christ, the Son of God.

Dietrich Bonhoeffer

Jesus said: 'Whoever accepts my commandments and obeys them is the one who loves me. My Father will love whoever loves me; I too will love him and reveal myself to him.'

John 14:21

*B*lessed are the peacemakers

Live in peace yourself and then you can bring peace to others.
Thomas à Kempis

Only those with nothing to defend can truly be peacemakers.
Jim Wallis

*Let us radiate the peace of God and so light his light and extinguish
in the world and in the hearts of all men all hatred, and love for
power.*
Mother Teresa

*We will not find peace in our generation until we learn anew that 'a
man's life consisteth not in the abundance of the things which he
possesseth', but in those inner treasures of the spirit which 'no thief
approacheth, neither moth corrupteth'.*
Martin Luther King Jnr

*The truly peaceful man is the man who makes peace; and in order to
make peace, he must spend his life on the battlefield, standing
between the combattants whom he works to reconcile . . . Christian
peace destroys the 'established disorder' and is realized only when
justice is accomplished.*
Louis Evely

*God's own peacemaking involved the blood of the cross; true
Christian peacemaking is painful and costly too.*
John Stott

*F*or they shall be called sons of God

Let us love one another; for love is of God, and he who loves is born of God and knows God.

1 John 4:7

Those who speak up for peace are God's very own. They remember that they too were once enemies of God, and they recall how God dealt with them: not by destroying them, but by reconciling them to himself and to one another. This is God's way, and to be God's children means to follow in God's way.

Jim Wallis

They are doing the very work which the Son of God began when he came to earth the first time, and which he will finish when he returns the second time.

J. C. Ryle

If thou hast peace in thyself, and lovest the peace of thy brethren . . . so is God, through Christ, at peace with thee; and thou his beloved son, and heir also.

William Tyndale

*B*lessed are those who are persecuted because of righteousness

If we are the children of God, we are but strangers and pilgrims here. This is not our home, we here have no abiding city; therefore we heed not the troubles or difficulties by the way, they will soon pass.

George Muller

The cross of Christ was the price of his obedience to God amid a rebellious world; it was suffering for having done right, for loving where others hated, for representing in the flesh the forgiveness and the righteousness of God among humanity, which was both less forgiving and less righteous. The cross of Christ was God's overcoming evil with good.

The cross of the Christian is then no different: it is the price of our obedience to God's love toward all others in a world ruled by hate. Such unflinching love for friend and foe alike will mean hostility and suffering for us, as it did for him.

John Howard Yoder

It would be surprising if Christians were not persecuted; for their very existence is an affront to human self-centredness, a reminder of the absolute claims that God makes upon men's lives and that so many want to ignore and forget.

C. E. B. Cranfield

Count it all joy, my brethren, when you meet various trials, for you know that the testing of your faith produces steadfastness. And let steadfastness have its full effect, that you may be perfect and complete, lacking in nothing.

James 1:2–4

For theirs is the kingdom of heaven

Take up your cross, then, and follow Jesus, and you will enter eternal life. He went before you, carrying his cross, and on the cross he died for you, so that you too should carry your cross . . . For if you share his death, you will also share his life. If you are with him in his suffering, you will be with him in his glory.

Thomas à Kempis

If we have died with him, we shall also live with him;
if we endure, we shall also reign with him;
if we deny him, he also will deny us.

2 Timothy 2:11–12

To share Christ's shame is a glorious privilege, to have his fellowship – though it be in the midst of flames – is to have fullness of joy, and to partake of his humiliation in this world is the pledge of participation in his glory in the world to come.

C. E. B. Cranfield

No pain, no palm; no thorns, no throne; no gall, no glory; no cross, no crown.

William Penn

Blessed is the man who endures trial, for when he has stood the test he will receive the crown of life which God has promised to those who love him.

James 1:12

Blessed are you when people insult you, persecute you and falsely say all kinds of evil against you because of me.

God seldom gives his people so sweet a foretaste of their future rest, as in their deep afflictions . . . Even the best saints seldom taste of the delights of God, pure, spiritual, unmixed joys, in the time of their prosperity, as they do in their deepest troubles.

Richard Baxter

I count everything as loss because of the surpassing worth of knowing Christ Jesus my Lord. For his sake I have suffered the loss of all things, and count them as refuse, in order that I may gain Christ and be found in him, not having a righteousness of my own, based on law, but that which is through faith in Christ, the righteousness from God that depends on faith; that I may know him and the power of his resurrection, and may share his sufferings, becoming like him in his death, that if possible I may attain the resurrection from the dead. Not that I have already obtained this or am already perfect; but I press on to make it my own, because Christ Jesus has made me his own. Brethren, I do not consider that I have made it my own; but one thing I do, forgetting what lies behind and straining forward to what lies ahead, I press on toward the goal for the prize of the upward call of God in Christ Jesus.

Philippians 3:8–14

Dear friends, do not be surprised at the painful trial you are suffering, as though something strange were happening to you. But rejoice that you participate in the sufferings of Christ, so that you may be overjoyed when his glory is revealed. If you are insulted because of the name of Christ, you are blessed, for the Spirit of glory and of God rests on you. If you suffer, it should not be as a murderer or thief or any other kind of criminal, or even as a meddler. However, if you suffer as a Christian, do not be ashamed, but praise God that you bear that name.

1 Peter 4:12–16

*R*ejoice and be glad, because great is your reward in heaven, for in the same way they persecuted the prophets who were before you.

We are children of God, and if children, then heirs, heirs of God and fellow heirs with Christ, provided we suffer with him in order that we may also be glorified with him. I consider that the sufferings of this present time are not worth comparing with the glory that is to be revealed to us.

Romans 8:17–18

Therefore, since we are surrounded by so great a cloud of witnesses, let us also lay aside every weight, and sin which clings so closely, and let us run with perseverance the race that is set before us, looking to Jesus the pioneer and perfecter of our faith, who for the joy that was set before him endured the cross, despising the shame, and is seated at the right hand of the throne of God. Consider him who endured from sinners such hostility against himself, so that you may not grow weary or faint-hearted.

Hebrews 12:1–3

Blessed be the God and Father of our Lord Jesus Christ! By his great mercy we have been born anew to a living hope through the resurrection of Jesus Christ from the dead, and to an inheritance which is imperishable, undefiled, and unfading, kept in heaven for you, who by God's power are guarded through faith for a salvation ready to be revealed in the last time. In this you rejoice, though now for a little while you may have to suffer various trials, so that the genuineness of your faith, more precious than gold which though perishable is tested by fire, may redound to praise and glory and honour at the revelation of Jesus Christ.

1 Peter 1:3–7

Sufferings are light, the glory infinite.

Francis of Assisi

Whoever wants to save his life will lose it, but whoever loses his life for me will save it.

Luke 9:24

Prayer

Lord, make me an instrument of thy peace. Where there is hatred, let me sow love; where there is injury, pardon; where there is doubt, faith; where there is despair, hope; where there is sadness, joy; where there is darkness, light.

O Divine Master, grant that I may not so much seek to be consoled, as to console; not so much to be understood, as to understand; not so much to be loved, as to love. For it is in giving that we receive, it is in pardoning that we are pardoned, it is in dying that we are born again to eternal life.

Francis of Assisi

Quotations from copyright material are as follows:
Augustine, The Confessions of Augustine in Modern English, translated by Sherwood E. Wirt, Zondervan Publishers 1971, Lion Publishing 1978; William Barclay, Matthew, Daily Study Bible, St Andrew Press; Dietrich Bonhoeffer, The Cost of Discipleship, SCM Press 1959; C. E. B. Cranfield, The First Epistle of Peter, SCM Press 1950; Louis Evely, Gospel Meditations, Doubleday and Company 1974, A. R. Mowbray 1975; Thomas à Kempis, The Imitation of Christ, translated by Betty I. Knott, Collins Fontana 1963; Martin Luther King Jnr, Strength to Love, Hodder and Stoughton 1964; Andrew Knowles, Now the Good News, Lion Publishing 1983; Brother Lawrence, The Practice of the Presence of God, E. M. Blaiklock, Hodder and Stoughton 1981; C. S. Lewis, Mere Christianity, Collins Fontana 1952; Martyn Lloyd-Jones, Studies in the Sermon on the Mount, Inter-Varsity Press 1959; John Stott, quote pages 19, 30, Christian Counter-culture, Inter-Varsity Press 1978, quote page 32, The New Abolitionists, Harper and Row 1983; Mother Teresa, quoted in Something Beautiful for God by Malcolm Muggeridge, Collins 1971; Jim Wallis quote pages 8, 35, The Call to Conversion, Harper and Row 1981, Lion Publishing 1982, quote page 32, Revive Us Again, Abingdon Press 1983, The New Radical, Lion Publishing 1983; John Howard Yoder, quoted in Waging Peace, Harper and Row 1983

Photographs by Sonia Halliday Photographs: F.H.C. Birch, pages 9, 22, Sonia Halliday, pages 18, 31, Jane Taylor, pages 14–15, 42–43; Gilly Huggett, page 41; R. W. G. Hunt, page 33; Lion Publishing: David Alexander, page 17, Jon Willcocks, pages 24, 28, 37; John Williams, page 39; Xenon: J. Simmons, page 11, Liba Taylor, page 12; ZEFA, pages 5, 21, 27, 34 and cover